By the Way

From Relational to Missional
John 14 –17

RANDY POOL

authorHOUSE®

AuthorHouse™
1663 Liberty Drive
Bloomington, IN 47403
www.authorhouse.com
Phone: 1 (800) 839-8640

Scripture quotations marked NKJV are taken from the New King James Version. Copyright © 1982 by Thomas Nelson, Inc. Used by permission. All rights reserved.

Scripture quotations marked AMP are from The Amplified Bible, Old Testament copyright © 1965, 1987 by the Zondervan Corporation. The Amplified Bible, New Testament copyright © 1954, 1958, 1987 by The Lockman Foundation. Used by permission. All rights reserved.

Published by AuthorHouse 01/05/2016

ISBN: 978-1-5049-7024-2 (sc)
ISBN: 978-1-5049-7023-5 (e)

Print information available on the last page.

Acknowledgements

The following book has been a work in progress for over twenty years. I first began sharing its truths while on the mission field of Central America. It grew out of necessity to explain with those we were ministering to concerning the "basics" of Christian living. For the past fifteen years, I have been sharing it faithfully in nearly every church I am asked to speak in on a Sunday morning. I prepared a shortened version that I could present during a Sunday School class and would faithfully ask for the opportunity to do so. I called the study *UNXNU* which stood for "You in Christ in you" (the *X* being the Greek letter *Chi* and representing *Christ*). This book is *UNXNU* on steroids.

I would like to acknowledge that many of the truths were gleaned throughout my own personal spiritual pilgrimage from the writings of men like Major Ian Thomas (now deceased) and it is inevitable that some expressions of his have become part of my thinking process and will appear in my communication of that truth. I am not trying to pirate him, his writings or his sermons, but know that his influence on my life has left its mark and if I use his phrasing, it is with the deepest respect of a disciple.

I would like to acknowledge my family as my greatest inspiration for wanting to finally record these truths. They have encouraged me more than they know by incorporating these truths into their own lives and their own presentation of the gospel. It is my joy to see others display that *Aha* moment, when they hear and discover how their relationship to Christ transforms the way God sees them as well as the way the world sees them.

Finally, I would like to acknowledge that my journey is far from over. This book deals with some foundational truths. The outworking of God in my life is still being discovered. I am still a *learner*. I am excited about what lies ahead as I travel *by the way*.

DEDICATION

Along the way, my ministry has been enhanced by the opportunities to teach from God's Word. There was a time in my life when that aspect of ministry became amazingly apparent and I felt incredibly fulfilled. By the way, it still does. I was in Honduras when I wrote my father a letter conveying that satisfaction as a teacher. He replied by writing me a letter that I will never forget. It was a strongly affirming letter and made a comparison I will never forget. My father said that I had begun one of the most aspiring vocations that was practiced by my Master, Jesus Christ – the aspect of teaching.

I would like to dedicate my first teaching work to my father, Herman Pool. He was a teacher of men in the armed forces and has taught me many life lessons. He is also a master story teller and much of what my writing reflects comes from listening to and emulating my father. I would like to honor him with this book. I love you, Dad.

INTRODUCTION

"*By the way…*" is usually accompanied by something we didn't want to forget to say. It is our way of inserting something we feel significant into a conversation. It is a self imposed interruption that many times changes our entire stream of thought. Whatever follows "*by the way,*" is important for the one speaking to communicate at that moment.

The Gospel of John, chapters 14 – 17 is a "*by the way*" for Jesus. Though he had been looking forward to celebrating the Passover with His disciples for a long time (Luke 22:15), the event itself had turned into a time of disappointment and confusion. During the meal, Jesus assumes the role that none of them would accept – a servant. Taking a towel and basin, he washes their feet (even Judas') and rebukes them for not having a servant heart already. Peter objects and then asks for a bath. He obviously has no idea what Jesus is doing.

Returning to the table Jesus stoically announces that one of them eating with him would betray him in accordance to the scriptures (Psalm 41:9). This is both troubling to the Master (John 13:22) and confusing to the disciples who begin to question among themselves of whom does he refer. The question is asked and answered. Jesus will identify the betrayer with a piece of bread. How ironic that the Bread of Life offers the bread of honor to his own betrayer and the bewildered disciples still miss it. He tells Judas to leave quickly before the others figure out the obvious. Judas leaves the meal to seal the deal and the rest think he's going out to do benevolence and make further arrangements for a celebration that none of them will experience. They have no idea what is going on.

With Judas gone, Jesus begins to feel the weight of the moment and begins to share what is really on his heart. His hour has come. It is all about to begin. It is now time to make sure that the ones he has shared his life with for three years understand that He is literally about to pour His life into them.

Calling them children in his own endearing way, Jesus tries to brace them for his departure once again. This time he adds a new dimension to the love He has been showing and commanding them to express. Whereas the law and prophets could be summarized with "loving your neighbor as yourself", Jesus now asks them to love one another "as He has loved them". It is not enough to love your neighbor with a humanitarian form of affection – a true disciple of Christ must love as Christ loved. And yet, they have no idea to the degree to which that love is about to be expressed.

Peter tries to cover the awkwardness of their confusion by asking *where* Jesus was about to go – rather than *what* He was about to do. Jesus explains that the where is not for him or the others *at this time*. This is a cup Jesus must drink alone. *Their* time will come. *By the way,* He is *not* talking about heaven – He's talking about His suffering. Peter takes the defensive stance and declares his *dying* devotion. But Jesus knows better. He peers deep into Peter's eyes as though to say, *"You have no idea what you are capable of!"* – He then prophesies that *before this night is over, you will deny me not once, not twice, but three times!* Talk about a slap in the face. Peter tries to reaffirm his commitment along with the rest of the disciples present, and though their voices sound strong, their promises are hollow (Matthew 26:35) for they have no idea what is going on.

Jesus looks around the room and sees the confusion and bewilderment in their eyes. This great celebration, that each of them has approached with great anticipation and excitement is collapsing around them. They did not understand about the washing of their feet. They did not understand about new meanings being given to the bread and the wine. They did not understand about the talk of a betrayer at the table. They did not understand where Jesus was about to go. They didn't understand how Peter could deny the Master. They did not understand most of what was happening around them and their faces revealed it. Looking into their troubled eyes, Jesus begins with words of comfort, *"Let not your heart be troubled, you believe in GOD – believe also in me."* And then as though He almost forgot to tell them, *"By the way, … in my Father's house, there are many places to dwell …"*

Stop right here and check something out. Open your Bible to John 14. If you have a *red letter edition* you are about to see something fascinating. Regardless of your translation, if your Bible records the words of Jesus in red – do the following: *Look* (don't read) at chapter *fourteen*. Now look at chapter *fifteen*. Now look at chapter *sixteen*. Now look at chapter *seventeen*. With the exception of a few interruptions, the four chapters are almost completely crimson. This is the longest single discourse given by the Lord. It is longer than the Sermon on the Mount – and for good reason – it is the last time Jesus will have with His disciples before His arrest, crucifixion and burial. For three years they have witnessed His miracles, signs and wonders. For three years they have heard his sermons, parables, and teachings. For three years, he has poured himself into this small band of fishermen, tax collectors, political activists, philosophers and crooks and for the most of that time, they have been clueless to who he was and what he was telling them. That which Jesus is about to say is of the utmost importance. It will begin in the upper room and follow them out into the night. He will continue teaching them along the dark roads of the countryside as they leave Jerusalem heading towards the Mount of Olives. It will culminate with a prayer of intercession and commission that he will direct to the Father in the presence of the disciples to underscore all that he has just told them. The discourse moves from relational to missional. It begins with their heavenly home, but moves quickly to their present purpose. And yet, it begins almost as an aside to what they have been discussing. As though, before they come ... before they take me ... before I am removed from among you and the passion begins ... there's something you need to know. So, *by the way . . . I AM the Way.*

By the way ... I am making The Way

By the way ... you will live your lives "by the Way"

By the way ... you will share Me with others . . . "along the way".

– Chapter One –

"Two Homes"

"Let not your heart be troubled; you believe in God, believe also in Me.

In My Father's house are many mansions; if it were not so, I would have told you. I go to prepare a place for you.

And if I go and prepare a place for you, I will come again and receive you to Myself; that where I am, there you may be also.

And where I go you know, and the way you know." **John 14:1- 3**[1]

Jesus answered and said to him, "If anyone loves Me, he will keep My word; and My Father will love him, and We will come to him and make Our home with him." **John 14:23**

In seeking to calm his bewildered disciples, Jesus immediately draws their thoughts to the Father above – the source of all comfort. Literally, he commands them to "stop letting their hearts to be troubled!" They were already agitated and confused and Jesus needed them to calm down. He commands them to trust both God the Father and himself (God, the Son). The correlation was about to become unquestionable. Even if it hadn't been obvious, Jesus was about to dispel all doubt. In the discourse to follow, Jesus will not only equate himself with the father, he will unveil the uniqueness of his relationship with the father that only one man has shared with God since Adam's fall. Before he describes that relationship that he shared with the father, he describes the two homes that he will share with the believer. The first is mentioned in verse two and the second in verse twenty-three.

In the opening verses, Jesus speaks of a dwelling place in the Father's house. We call it a mansion. We sing about it from great hymns such as "Victory in Jesus" to Elvis Presley's "In My Father's House (There are Many Mansions)". We use the imagery to contrast our lot in life in this world to the day when we will be blessed beyond measure. We look forward to the day when we trade off these rags for God's riches. In many ways, we have made our "home in heaven" the motivation for giving ones life to Jesus.

Most presentations of the gospel will make heaven the prize for coming to Christ. We ask, "Do you know that if you were to die today (tonight) that you would spend eternity with God *in heaven*?" Or we ask, "if you were to stand before God at the gate to *heaven* and He should ask you 'why I should let you into my Kingdom', what would you say?" We speak of the "Highway to *heaven*", the "Roman Road to *heaven*", even Jesus – the only way *to heaven*.

Not that there is anything wrong with those questions or presentations – but if heaven is *all* we present, then we are only sharing half of the message. If you tear a one hundred dollar bill in half – you don't have two fifties – you have nothing. A presentation of salvation that only offers a "home in heaven" is only half a presentation. John fourteen speaks of *two homes* not just one.

In the process of explaining the changing role of the coming Holy Spirit (which we will get to in greater detail in a later chapter), Jesus mentions that to those who love him and the father - he (Jesus) will disclose (or manifest) himself. Judas (not Iscariot) asks an interesting question that is not directly addressed by Jesus' response. However, what Jesus does indicate adds a whole new dimension to the relationship they are about to share. Just seconds earlier, Jesus introduced to his disciples that the Holy Spirit would be moving from visitor to residence status stating, *"the Spirit of truth, whom the world cannot receive, because it neither sees Him nor knows Him; but you know Him, for He dwells with you and <u>will be in you</u>. ."* The difference between the activity of the Holy Spirit of the Old Testament and what would happen after Pentecost had to do with the permanent presence of the Spirit of God *within* the God fearer and not just *upon* them for anointed purposes.

Judas asks, *"Lord, how is it that You will manifest Yourself to us, and not to the world?"* (vs. 22). The question reflects the confusion over what Jesus is telling them, but more than that, it suggests that the disciples had missed something that had *already* happened. Jesus has been speaking in the future tense up to this time, and yet, Judas is correct. They had missed something. To be honest, they had been clueless most of the three years that they had walked with the Son of God. When Peter finally blurted out the correct answer of Christ's identity at Caesarea Philippi (Matthew 16:16), he still didn't understand what it meant. For this reason, Jesus strongly instructed Peter and the others to *not* tell anyone that He was the Christ, the Son of the Living God (Matthew 16:20). It's one thing to know that Jesus is the Son of God and another to know what that means. The disciples had missed a great deal during their time with the Master, and now it was becoming evident. So Judas finally asks the question.

Jesus responds with the greatest revelation that man would ever receive. More important than Peter's "confession of faith" is the revelation of what that "confession" would realize – that the God who created us actually desires to dwell in us (and always has) – permanently. Even the terminology that Jesus used was significant. Jesus said, *"If anyone loves Me, he will keep My word; and My Father will love him, and We will come to him and make Our home with him."* (John 14:23) Would it surprise you to learn that the word "*home*" is the same word translated "*mansion*" in verse two? It is the noun *monē* and means "a residence" or "dwelling place". Jesus was saying, "I am going to prepare a place for you (verse 2), but in the meantime, you are going to be preparing a place for ME (verse 23), so that wherever you are, I will be also!"

The great promise of a home in heaven someday was to be understood in light of the promise of a home in them on earth TODAY! We call the home that Jesus is preparing us a "mansion". Paul will later describe the home we are preparing for him in our own bodies as a "temple" (1 Corinthians 6:19, 20). It is not unreasonable to suggest that there is no "mansion" without a "temple". If we are not prepared to give Him a place in our life to express Himself through (a temple), we shouldn't expect Him to prepare a place for us when this life has passed.

I realize this begs the age-old question of whether you can receive Jesus as Savior without receiving Him as Lord. I believe the answer to that is clear – we just prefer to default to the expressions we have come to learn and repeat when sharing the gospel. Let it suffice for now that the scriptures do not present a Savior who some-day may become your Lord, but a Lord Who can be your Savior today. Romans 10, Philippians 2, and a host of other scriptures instruct us to call upon the name of the "LORD" and His name is *Jesus*.

Just look at the title: *Savior, Jesus Christ* appears but six times in three books (2 Timothy, Titus, and 2 Peter) of the New Testament. *Lord Jesus Christ* appears eighty times in twenty books of the New Testament. Use simply *Lord Jesus* and you add another thirty six times and two more books. In short, *Lord Jesus* occurs 116 times in twenty- two New Testament books to the six times you find the title *Savior Jesus Christ*. How do you think He wants to be received or presented?

An individual is defined by their title not their job description. If you think I am nit-picking over semantics, see if the groom at the next wedding you attend vows to take "this woman to be my lawfully wedded dish-washer." Jesus is our Savior, but that is not the basis upon which we receive Him, nor is it the basis upon which He receives us. As a husband takes a bride – He has taken us – to know us intimately and to protect us from harm (and sin) by laying down His own life for us. Let us not trample His death by refusing His life and Lordship.

We don't receive forgiveness or a Savior – we receive *JESUS*, the Son of God and Lord of all *and* He forgives to us our sins by separating us from them and their consequences (death) thereby becoming our Savior.

A relationship with Christ is about two homes – yours and His. *You don't get a mansion without becoming a temple.* For you to someday dwell with Him – He must dwell in you TODAY. And we don't receive Him into our "home" as a guest, but as the *landLORD* of all. It will take time for you both to become comfortable with the arrangement – that is the process of sanctification, but the Lord is patient. He will fill every area of our life that we yield – but it begins with the acknowledgement that He is already Lord of those areas, whether we act like it or not. Robert Boyd Munger has written a tremendous work illustrating the process of how Jesus makes Himself *at home* within our lives. I strongly recommend *"My Heart, Christ's Home"*[2] for every new believer. And for those who were unaware of the two homes, it would be great reading as well.

It has not been my intention to put doubts in the hearts of those who may have prayed to receive Christ as their *"personal Savior"*. The proof of a true believer is not the words they prayed, but the heart from which they prayed. Romans 10:13 says, "For *whoever calls on the name of the Lord shall be saved.*" It doesn't give us the words with which to call upon His name. There is no magical prayer. It could be as simple as the publican who beat his chest and cried, *"God, be merciful to me a sinner!"*, or as lengthy as the man who cries out from his personal burden of sin and begins confessing them before God. It is not what you say as much as it is what you mean.

By the way, ... He knows when you mean it or not.

– Chapter Two –

"The Two Interruptions"
[John 14:3-31]

Back in the upper room, Jesus has just announced His preparations for a home in heaven. He then adds *salt* to the discourse. You have heard it said, *"you can lead a horse to water, but you can't make him drink"*. A wise man once added, *"but you can salt his oats and make him thirsty"*! If you want to get others involved in what you are saying, then *salt* the conversation with something that provokes a question on their part.

Jesus said, *"And where I go you know, and the way you know."* To which the red letters cease and Thomas mutters through the first of two interruptions, *"Lord, we do not know where You are going, and how can we know the way?"* Jesus responds with the verse that most of us memorized to affirm the uniqueness of Jesus Christ as the *only* way to the Father - *"Jesus said to him, "I am the way, the truth, and the life. No one comes to the Father except through Me."*

Without exception, this statement is the tipping point of Christianity. It leaves no room for compromise or inclusion of any other person or system of belief to bring us before the presence of our Creator. Without Christ, you can't even *know* the Father (John 17:3) let alone enter His eternal Kingdom. Those three words embody the essence of our relationship with God.

Jesus is *The Way*. He is more than the *way* for us to return to the Father – He is also the *way* for the Father to return to us. You see, it is not a matter of *reaching* the Father. It is a matter of *returning* to the Father. Most presentations of the Gospel begin with a post-fallen man stating the present condition of human depravity through verses such as Romans 3:10, 23. For us to understand the gospel as our *return* to the Father, we must first see from whence we wandered. The prodigal son was *lost*, only in the sense that he was not where he belonged. He was *found* when he was restored to the place where he belonged. The story doesn't begin in the pig pen and neither does ours.

> *God made man in order to have a meaningful relationship with him. This was to be an intimate relationship of fellowship and worship that would make man complete and whole* (Genesis 1:26 – 31; Psalm 139:13 – 18; Revelation 4:11; Romans 11:36).

It was not enough to create life. The earth was full of plant life, sea life, and animal life. Then God decided to create life that could share His life. He breathed into man His own Spirit (Genesis 2:7) and then communed with man through his (man's) spirit – "*And they heard the voice of the LORD God walking in the garden in the cool* (ruach – spirit) *of the day*" (Genesis 3:8). This was later confirmed by Jesus to the Samaritan woman in John 4 – "*God is a Spirit: and they that worship him must worship him in spirit and in truth*" (John 4:24). That was *the way* God made man – to be indwelt by the Spirit of God in order to have fellowship and worship and to make man whole and complete.

> **Man believed the lie that he could have a meaningful life apart from God** *(Genesis 3:1-7; John 8:44).*

Many times, that which is worse than telling a lie is believing a lie. You can tell a lie and know that you have done wrong, but you can believe a lie and suffer consequences you never intended or expected. This is not to excuse Adam and Eve, for in order to believe the lie of the serpent they had to disregard the Word of the Lord. That is where all sin begins. Satan offered wisdom, knowledge, and divinity in exchange for simple disobedience to God. But there is nothing simple in disobedience – regardless of the apparent lack of seriousness of the activity. Who would have thought that a simple act of eating a single fruit would result in the cursing of a planet and the eternal destruction of the human race. But it was not the act that condemned them, it was a belief. "I can have a meaningful life without God!" they believed. The act demonstrated their belief. Even sin is based on faith – faith that nothing bad will come from it. They were wrong. When you believe a lie – faith and sincerity are misplaced and you will suffer the consequences.

> *Man exchanged his relationship with God for a life of self-centered meaningless activity through sin* (*Romans 1:22 – 25*).

Adam and Eve lost more than fellowship, they lost their relationship with their Creator. The Spirit of God withdrew and they were driven from the garden and away from His presence. Now they were on their own. God could cover their sin with animal skins in a foreshadow of His future atonement in Christ, but there was still a price to be paid. That price was not just the death that their sin would cause, but also the life that their sin would produce – a life of self-centered meaningless activity and existence – what Solomon would later call *vanity of vanities* (complete emptiness). Man now had a hole in his soul where God used to dwell. For the centuries to follow, he would try every means possible to fill the void, but would never succeed.

> *Now all men are born separated from God and bent on self-destruction because of sin* (*Genesis 5:3; Romans 3:10, 23; 5:12 - 19; 6:23; James 1:14, 15*).

The proof that all men sin is the fact that all men die. When Adam exchanged his relationship with God for an existence apart from God through disobedience, he passed his condition on to all who would follow him. From Genesis 5, man was no longer seen by either God or man to reflect the image of his creator. Instead, he reflected the image of his fallen father – Adam. With this distorted image came a death sentence that took place both immediately (spiritually) and eventually (physically). The physical death verified the spiritual death. Had Adam and Eve not sinned, they would not have died. The holistic consequence of sin is death – both physically and spiritually.

There was only *one way* to change the result of sin upon mankind. There was only *one way* to restore the lost relationship between God and man.

> ***Jesus came as the God/man to restore the broken relationship between man and his creator.*** *(John 1:1-12; 3:16; Colossians 1:15-20; Hebrews 1:1-3; 1 Timothy 2:3-6).*

God became a man. There is no debating the Deity (not just divinity) of Jesus Christ. Divinity suggests a spark of the divine, but Deity declares the total equality of Being from within the Godhead now in human flesh (Colossians 2:9). God became a man and His name was Jesus of Nazareth. If He were only man, He would have shared the stain of sin. If He were only God, He could not have died in our place. His life proved He was God, His death proved He was man, and His resurrection proves He is Lord. He did not come to *show* the way.

He came to *be* the Way. *By the way*, the early church even took on the title of "the Way" (Acts 9:2; 19:9, 23; 22:4; 24:14, 22).

Jesus is *The Truth*. He didn't just speak the truth – though everything He said was true. He embodied the truth. As the God/man, he was the truth about both. Major Ian Thomas put it succinctly, "Jesus is the truth about man and the truth about God. He is the truth about man because he is the truth about God. Because the truth about God is that God made man to be the truth about God" (preached during Spring Bible Conference 1976 at Union University in Jackson, TN). Jesus was the visible image of the invisible God in everything He said and did. This is why He could say unequivocally, "If you have seen me – you have seen the Father." (which we will examine next).

According to Paul, man had exchanged *the truth* of God for a lie (*Romans 1:25*). Jesus came as the *truth* of God to overcome the lie and to undo the damage that the lie had caused. In a world that chides absolute truth, Jesus came to declare that He was absolutely the *truth. By the way,* only a liar would deny that! (*1 John 2:22*)

Jesus is *The Life*. The truth is that Jesus is the only way because He is the *life* that was lost in Adam. Just run through the verses concerning "*life*" in the writings of John and see what you find:

- *In him (Jesus) was life; and the life was the light of men.* John 1:4
- *For as the Father has life in Himself, so He has granted the Son to have life in Himself;* John 5:26
- *You search the Scriptures, for in them you think you have eternal life; and these are they which testify of Me.* John 5:39
- *For the bread of God is He who comes down from heaven and gives life to the world."*
  …"I am the bread of life…. John 6:33ff
- *I have come that they may have life, and that they may have it more abundantly.* John 10:10
- *Jesus said to her, "I am the resurrection and the life. He who believes in Me, though he may die, he shall live.* John 11:25
- *This is eternal life, that they may know You, the only true God, and Jesus Christ whom You have sent.* John 17:3
- *But these are written that you may believe that Jesus is the Christ, the Son of God, and that believing you may have life in His name.* John 20:31
- *He who has the Son has life; he who does not have the Son of God does not have life.*
  These things I have written to you who believe in the name of the Son of God, that you may know that you have eternal life, and that you may continue to believe in the name of the Son of God. 1 John 5:12, 13

We don't receive eternal life through believing in Jesus – we receive JESUS and He *is the life* we receive. Eternal life is *knowing* Him! *By the way,* that *life* begins the moment we receive Him.

For Jesus to use these three terms that night was far more than the disciples could digest. It would take more than the weekend to fully comprehend the depth of His words. He was the Way because He was the Truth. He was the Truth because He was the Life. And because He was the Life – He is now the Way. Got it! They didn't … not that night. So He continued to speak.

"If you had known Me, you would have known My Father also; and from now on you know Him and have seen Him." (John 14:7)

The room goes quiet. The disciples all look at one another except for Philip. His eyes widen. This is what he has been waiting for. He rushes forward with the second interruption of the night.

Philip said to Him, "Lord, show us the Father, and it is sufficient for us." (John 14:8)

This was not the first time that the disciples had been clueless to their surroundings or to what Jesus was doing or saying. Many a time, I can imagine Jesus cocking his head to one side, taking a deep breath and heaving a deep sigh. This was one of those times. You can almost hear the frustration in his voice as he exhales the words:

> *"Have I been with you so long, and yet you have not known Me, Philip? He who has seen Me has seen the Father; so how can you say, 'Show us the Father'? Do you not believe that I am in the Father, and the Father in Me? The words that I speak to you I do not speak on My own authority; but the Father who dwells in Me does the works.*
>
> John 14:9, 10

It is the response to this second interruption where Jesus is able to unfold the nature of His relationship with His Father and what will be the basis of our union with Him. This is not the first time He will speak of this special dual relationship. In defending His deity before the Jews wishing to stone Him, He affirmed, *"If I do not do the works of My Father, do not believe Me; but if I do, though you do not believe Me, believe the works, that you may know and believe that the <u>Father is in Me, and I in Him</u>"* (John 10:37, 38).

He then explains that everything they had seen and heard for the past three years had its origin in the Father. The sermons, the parables, the quick responses to Pharisaical challenges, and even the revealing "I am" declarations were not spoken on His own accord, but found their origin in the one Who had sent Him. The miracles, the signs, the wonders, the healings were all done by the Father through the hands of the Son.

Earlier that year He had tried to explain that, in and of Himself (that is in His flesh), "He could do ... *nothing!*" (John 5:19, 30). The Father in Him did the work and deserved the glory.

For the first time since Adam, there has been a man on earth fully indwelt by the Father in Heaven. That is why Paul will refer to Jesus as both the "last Adam" (1 Corinthians 15:45) and the "second man" two verses later (1 Corinthian 15:47):

> *And so it is written, "The first man Adam became a living being." The <u>last Adam</u> became a life-giving spirit. However, the spiritual is not first, but the natural, and afterward the spiritual.*
>
> *The first man was of the earth, made of dust; the <u>second Man</u> is the Lord from heaven.*
>   I Corinthians 15:45-47

He is the second man, in that He is only the second man to walk this earth as God intended man to be – fully indwelt by God. He is the last Adam, in that there will be no more like Him to ever come again. No other man can claim Sonship from God in the manner that Jesus can. No one! The uniqueness of Jesus Christ is summarized by this one statement – *"I am in the Father and the Father is in me!"*

For nearly the remainder of this chapter, Jesus begins to talk about the coming of the Holy Spirit, but they are not ready for that yet. No more than Peter was ready for the impact of his great profession of faith recorded in Matthew 16. While in Caesarea Philippi, Jesus asked the disciples what they had been hearing about Him. "Who do the people say that I am?" He asked. They replied with the rumors of the day, "Some say John the Baptist (who was already dead), some Elijah, or Jeremiah, or one of the prophets." So much for guessing, Jesus thought. Then came the loaded question, "Who do *you* say that I am?" It is not enough to form an opinion or agree with the polls concerning Christ. It really doesn't matter what others say or think. Nor is knowing who Jesus is the same as knowing Jesus. It is not about getting the answer right.

Peter exploded, *"You are the Christ – the Son of the Living God!"* Jesus smiled, *"Very good Peter! You are absolutely right! In fact, you have been listening to my Father, because flesh and blood didn't reveal this to you."* And then Jesus proceeded to pronounce one of the greatest blessings upon Peter that was ever recorded. But note His final comment – *"Then He commanded His disciples that they should tell no one that He was Jesus the Christ"* (Matthew 16:20).

Now why would He do that? Finally, one of the twelve understands for the first time who Jesus really is and Jesus tells him and the rest to keep it to themselves. That seems like just the opposite of the "Great Commission". The fact is, that although Peter understood (from God) *who* Jesus was – he still didn't understand what that meant. He didn't understand *why*

He came, *what* He was about to do, and *how* that would make a difference to the world around them. We know this because of the *next three verses*:

> *From that time Jesus began to show to His disciples that He must go to Jerusalem, and suffer many things from the elders and chief priests and scribes, and be killed, and be raised the third day. Then Peter took Him aside and began to rebuke Him, saying, "Far be it from You, Lord; this shall not happen to You!" But He turned and said to Peter, "Get behind Me, Satan! You are an offense to Me, for you are not mindful of the things of God, but the things of men."*
>
> Matthew 16:21-23

Armed with the knowledge that Jesus was the Christ, the Son of the Living God was not enough for Peter to understand the Gospel of His pending death, burial and resurrection. He couldn't connect the dots. It isn't the knowledge of sound doctrine that saves – it is knowing Jesus as something more than the master teacher, the prophet, or even the Son of God.

Back in the upper room, the disciples are starting to become more confused. Their understanding of the Holy Spirit is somewhat limited. There hasn't been a lot of talk about Him before now. This is something new. Jesus recognizes the limitations of their understanding and changes gears. He brings them back to the events of the night itself by announcing that His betrayal is soon and the "ruler of this world" (Satan) is on his way. Abruptly He closes the Seder, and as they sing (Matthew 26:30) the final portion of the Hallel (Psalms 115-118), Jesus invites them to leave the upper room and to head out into the night.

"Arise, let us go from here" - So they got up and left.

– Chapter Three –

"Two Points of View"
[John 15:1-5]

"I am the true vine, and My Father is the vinedresser.

Every branch in Me that does not bear fruit He takes away; and every branch that bears fruit He prunes, that it may bear more fruit.

You are already clean because of the word which I have spoken to you.

Abide in Me, and I in you. As the branch cannot bear fruit of itself, unless it abides in the vine, neither can you, unless you abide in Me.

"I am the vine, you are the branches. He who abides in Me, and I in him, bears much fruit; for without Me you can do nothing.

John 15:1-5

With a determination that none understood, Jesus rose from the table and without hesitation made His way through the door and into the night. But He was not through with His final address to the (now) eleven that obediently followed behind. Chapter fifteen continues without a pause in thought. Some have suggested that

Jesus used either a hillside vineyard or the bronze vine alongside the Temple wall (representing Israel) to be the springboard for His next discourse. It does not matter what object lesson He may have used – it is the lesson itself that is important.

As Jesus continued to instruct His confused disciples, He went one step further in explaining the nature of the relationship He was about to share with each of them. In *John 15:1-5*, He shifts gears to explain that the relationship He had enjoyed and shared with the Father while in human flesh, was the same relationship that they would enjoy and share with Him.

> *"I am the true vine, and My Father is the vinedresser.*
>
> *Every branch in Me that does not bear fruit He takes away; and every branch that bears fruit He prunes, that it may bear more fruit.*
>
> *You are already clean because of the word which I have spoken to you.*
>
> *Abide in Me, and I in you. As the branch cannot bear fruit of itself, unless it abides in the vine, neither can you, unless you abide in Me.*
>
> *"I am the vine, you are the branches. He who abides in Me, and I in him, bears much fruit; for without Me you can do nothing.* John 15:1-5

Just as apart from the Father, Christ could do nothing in and of Himself, now apart from Him they would be able to do nothing in and of themselves. Just as Christ was "in the Father", they would be placed "in Him". To become a Christian would mean these two glorious truths: I am in Christ and He is in me.

Though the manner in which many would come to know the Risen Lord may differ, the final result would be the same universally: the believer would be placed in Christ and Christ would indwell the believer. When we understand the import of these two truths, so much of the scripture becomes clear. Error tends to surface where truth has been distorted. Truth out of balance with itself is the most subtle of all error. Many groups have strayed into error by over-emphasizing one of these two truths over the other. Allow me to digress enough to illustrate.

I once asked a group of Honduran pastors to indicate something for me. I first asked how many were "children of God"? As part of God's forever family and counted among the redeemed, they all raised their hands enthusiastically and exclaimed, "Amen!" (which is the same in Spanish as it is in English). I then asked the same group to lift their hand, those who were children of God by being "*born*" into the family of God. Most raised their hands while others waited to see if the question was a trap or not. I then asked for those who were children of God through "*adoption*" to raise their hand. The cautious group smiled widely and shot up their hands while the first group began to lower theirs. Then a few began to reconsider and asked if they could change their minds. I agreed and presented both questions a second time with equal emphasis. Now the group began to snicker and chatter amongst themselves debating which was more appropriate. I could hear verses being quoted back and forth. I then offered the following solution. I asked those who had been "born" in the family of God to lift their left hand, and those who had been "adopted" into the family of God to lift their right hand. Amidst laughter and relief, the classroom responded unanimously by lifting both hands into the air. I then asked, why couldn't they have just done so in the beginning. The question wasn't a preference between two choices, it was an acknowledgement of two truths.

Paul uses "adoption" (*Romans, Galatians, and Ephesians*) to show our "placement" in the Body of Christ. John (*John 3; 1 John*) speaks of being "born of God" to show the regenerative purpose of Christ indwelling the believer. One term presents our "position", while the other speaks of an ongoing "experience". Through "adoption", we are placed "in Christ". Through being "born of God", Christ enters our humanity and begins to conform us into His image.

The Bible uses many terms to describe these two aspects of salvation. Adoption and being born are just two of them. Just as they present two sides to the same coin, so do the other expressions. Jesus chose to use two statements to describe the relationship that His followers would share with Him. They would be *in Him* and He would be *in them* – just as He had been *in the Father* and the Father was *in Him*.

In the moment I gave my life to Christ, two wonderful truths took place in my life. I was fifteen years old and in response to my simple prayer of repentance and faith, I was placed *in Christ* and that would forever change the way God would see me. At the same moment, Christ came in to dwell *in me* through the person of the Holy Spirit and *that* would change the way the world would see me. These two points of view change the moment Jesus comes into your life. Let's look at those two points of view.

YOU IN CHRIST - Changes the Way God see you

Over one hundred and twenty five times, Paul uses the expression "in Christ", or "in Him" or something similar to describe a position of justification whereby God no longer sees us in our sins, but rather sees us clothed with the very righteousness of Christ. *Ephesians 1:5, 6* is one of the clearer passages.

Having predestined us to adoption as sons by Jesus Christ to Himself, according to the good pleasure of His will, to the praise of the glory of His grace, by which He made us accepted in the Beloved. Ephesians 4:5,6

Only one person has ever been "approved" by God – His Beloved Son, Jesus Christ. On two separate occasions the Father declared His approval from heaven stating, "This is my Beloved Son, in Whom I am well pleased" (*Matthew 3:17; 17:5*). Sinful man will never find the approval Christ attained, based on his own merit or self-righteousness. Therefore the only way to be found pleasing to God is to be "accepted" IN THE BELOVED! Through repentance of sin and faith in Christ, we can be "accepted", though we could never have ever been "approved". This acceptance is based on Christ's righteousness. In Him, God looks at us and sees Christ. We are clothed with the very righteousness of Christ. That is how we can be accepted.

*For He (*the Father*) made Him (*the Son*) who knew no sin to be sin for us, that we might become the righteousness of God in Him.* 2 Corinthians 5:21

Jesus removed the barrier of separation between man and God (sin and death) through His own death and resurrection (*Romans 5:6–8; 1 Corinthians 15:3, 4; Colossians 2:13–15; Ephesians 2:14–16; Hebrews 12:2*).

As difficult as it for me to comprehend (as well as try to explain), when Jesus Christ hung upon the cross of Calvary, God literally looked down upon His righteous Son and *saw* a wretched sinner. He was *made* sin for us and that is why the Father had to turn away as Jesus cried out, *"My God, my God, why have you forsaken me?"*

The second part of the verse proclaims an equally confounding truth. Just as God could look upon His righteous Son and see a wretched sinner, *in Christ*, God can now look upon me (a wretched sinner) and see a righteous son. That is too incredible for words.

If this was the only result of receiving Christ, it would be more than worth shouting about. To be seen clean before my Creator is more than I could ever hope to accomplish in my own efforts. My life and works would fall so short of the *image* of a Holy God (or as Paul would put it – the *glory of God* – in **Romans 3:23**. Now God sees me in a way that even my closest friend or family member can't. He sees me *righteous*! That alone is grace beyond my understanding – but good news – there is more!

> *Man can receive the relationship he lost with God through Jesus Christ (and Jesus Christ only) – (John 14:6; 17:1-3; Acts 4:10-12; Philippians 2:9-11; 1 John 5:11-13).*

CHRIST IN YOU – changes the way the world will see you.

It is the transforming nature of the Divine presence in the man. The Spirit is the means by which Christ "dwells in our hearts by faith" (*Ephesians 3:17*). One cannot have Christ without the Spirit (*Romans 8:9*). At the same moment the believer is *"accepted"* by God in Jesus Christ, the Spirit of Christ brings life to their human spirit and regenerates them. The indwelling Spirit then begins a lifetime of conforming this new creation into the image of Christ. The reality of Jesus Christ entering into the very life of the new believer must be embraced.

As we have already noticed, Jesus anticipates this reality and is excited about the possibilities. He *wants* to make His home in you. *Jesus answered and said to him, "If anyone loves Me, he will keep My word; and My Father will love him, and We will come to him and make Our home with him.* (John 14:23). One of the most incredible truths of the Good News is that the Creator would take residence within His creation in order to complete them. Volumes of theology have been written about the redemptive and regenerative act of God through Jesus Christ. I would be amiss to presume to abridge that wondrous truth. At the risk of oversimplifying God's greatest miracle and act of grace, allow me to make a few theological observations…again.

God made man to reflect His image – His character. He breathed His Spirit into the first man, Adam, giving him both life and the ability to reflect the image of God. Adam chose sin and consequently lost both his "spiritual" life (the ability to reflect the image of God) as well as his physical life (eventually). Every man born into this world no longer bears the image of God, but the image of sinful man – *in Adam*. Jesus came as the

express image of God. He possessed the "spiritual" life
that Adam forfeited and was lacking in man. His death
and resurrection removed the barrier of sin and allowed
man access to God. Those who receive Christ through
repentance and faith – receive the life that Adam lost
as well as the ability to reflect the image of God. This
is all made possible by the entrance of the Holy Spirit
into the human soul. That is why a person can't receive
Christ without the Spirit. Going to heaven is a by-
product of "knowing" God. Salvation is to restore man
to the purpose for which he was created – to reflect the
image of God.

> **God will restore man to the condition he
> originally planned in creation and will
> establish an ongoing (eternal) intimate
> relationship of fellowship and worship with
> him that will make him complete and whole
> (John 10:9, 10; 14:23; Romans 8:31-39;
> Galatians 5:22, 23; Ephesians 3:17-19).**

As we begin to live in the fellowship of this intimate
communion, it will change the way we behave. Christ
in you will affect the way people around you see you.
Those closest to us will see the difference that a new
nature can make as we die to self and allow the Spirit
of Christ to live His life through us.

> **Man must repent (change his mind/ heart
> about living a self-centered life) and believe
> that Jesus can both remove his sin and fill his**

> **life with His very presence in order to have**
> **a meaningful relationship with God** *(Acts*
> *20:20, 21; Romans 10:8-13).*

Paul describes this life exchange in his letter to the Galatians. In a classic passage memorized by many, Paul declares: *"I have been crucified with Christ* (self-denial)*; it is no longer I who live, but Christ lives in me* (through the indwelling Holy Spirit)*; and the life which I now live in the flesh I live by faith in the Son of God, who loved me and gave Himself for me* (Galatians 2:20). It has been noted by many that there is only one who can live the Christian life – Christ Himself. This verse bears that out. The question is *how*? How does Christ live His life through us? If you only memorized verse twenty, you would be quick to answer – "by *faith*". But that is only half of the answer. The second half lies in the first part of verse twenty-one - "I do not *set aside the grace* of God" (Galatians 2:21a). The Amplified Version reads, "[Therefore, I do not treat God's gracious gift as something of minor importance and defeat its very purpose]; I do not set aside and invalidate and frustrate and nullify the grace (unmerited favor) of God." That is not exaggerated, just amplified. It also clarifies that the *way* to live the Christian life is the same *way* you become a Christian in the first place – *by grace through faith.*[3]

Paul says that he lives *by faith* not frustrating *the grace.* This leads us to ask the question, *"what grace?"* If we define grace (as did the Amplified Version) as strictly "unmerited favor", we will have described the gift by its packaging alone. Grace is definitely a "gift from God" that we do not deserve, but that just makes it a package with my name on it. When I open the gift and look inside, what do I find? This is the key to *being the Christian you have become*. To understand and embrace the grace that God extends every day – the grace to be a new person in Christ.

The best illustration of grace is found in the single miracle that is recorded in all four gospels apart from the Passion Week. It is the "feeding of the five thousand". Mark's account sets the stage well (read Mark 6:30 and following). The disciples had just returned from their own mission trip with excitement and enthusiasm over the response of the people and the reaction of the demons. They had preached repentance, cast out demons and healed the sick. They were exhilarated, exhausted and famished. Jesus took note and prescribed a "time apart" before they "came apart". They pushed off from the shore to escape the crowds only to find that the crowds followed on foot along the shoreline keeping watch on where their boat was headed. As the group of fans traveled around the lake, they must have picked up others snowballing into a sizable mob. By the time the boat reached the opposite shore, this gathering was met by the curious on the other side and a multitude of over five thousand men plus women and children were waiting to greet the ship.

Peter jumps out of the boat and begins to tie the rope to a rock when he looks over his shoulder, sees this multitude and whispers to himself, "You have GOT to be kidding! We just left half of these people on the other side. Don't they know it is our DAY OFF!" But Jesus steps out of the boat, looks at the people and Mark records what Matthew will echo in another context: *"When He looked upon the multitudes, He was moved with compassion, for they were weary and faint, like sheep not having a shepherd."* Jesus sees people different than we do. The disciples looked upon the multitude and saw a nuisance. Jesus looked at the same people and saw need. God's perspective is so different than ours. Christ in you will cause you to begin to see what He sees – the *way* He sees it. Jesus sat the people down and began to teach them many things.

Keep in mind that the reason the Master suggested the trip and moved the disciples across the lake was because they had been so busy that there had not been time for them *to eat*. Now they sat for an afternoon message that lasted most of the day. When they could wait no longer, the disciples came to Jesus and interrupted Him to say that the day was spent and that it was time to eat. *Send the people away* so that they can go buy themselves some food. What they were really saying was "send the people away so *we* can get something to eat!"

The words that followed were unexpected and for the most part unwanted. Jesus looked the disciples square in the eyes and commanded, *"YOU give them something to eat!*" He already knew what He was going to do, He just wanted to see how they would respond to the command.

Bear in mind that Jesus seldom asks of us what we *can* do, because if He did, we would be able to do it *without* Him. He tends to ask us to do what we cannot do in order to drive us to Himself, so that He can do *through* us what we had neither the desire nor the ability to do on our own. In fact, the two main reasons why most believers do not act like believers when they are not around other believers are these: "*I don't want to! I know what the Bible says to do and to be honest, I just don't want to do it!*" The other may come across less defiant. "*You don't understand, I have TRIED and I just CAN'T DO IT!*" One speaks of a lack of desire and the other of a lack of ability. What Jesus offers is what we lack – the desire and ability.

Look into the disciples eyes again. They can't believe their ears. "*We came here to get away from the crowds, so we could finally get something to eat. You have spent the day teaching them and now you want us to feed them! Even if we wanted to, we don't have what it takes – conservatively, it would cost over eight months wages for everyone to get just a little. Where are we supposed to buy that much bread ... and with what? - Lord, face it. We can't do this!*"

Jesus looked back and must have smirked. He already knew what He was going to do next and they didn't! This was one of those tests that you look back on and try to smile to keep from crying. When we say – "*We can't!*" I believe, if you are sincere and listening to

God, you will Him say "*I never said you could, but I can, and I always said I would.*" That *is GRACE*! - when God gives you the two things that you lack in completing His will – desire and ability. In fact, Paul records for us a Biblical definition for grace without mentioning the term.

In Philippians 2:12 and 13, Paul writes, "*Therefore, my beloved, as you have always obeyed, not as in my presence only, but now much more in my absence, work out your own salvation with fear and trembling; for it is God who works in you both to will and to do for His good pleasure.*" In verse twelve, he instructs us to "work out our own salvation". This, of course isn't referring to "working *for* our salvation", but rather, living a life that demonstrates the salvation you have received in Jesus Christ. He then gives the secret as to how that life is to be lived – "for it is *God who works in you* both to will (desire) and to do (ability) for His good pleasure." Paul makes clear that the dynamic of the Christian life is the life of Christ *in* the believer providing both the *desire* ("to will") and the *ability* ("to do") to please God. That is Grace. Christ working *in* us to produce the *desire* and *ability* of His own will.

The old adage of WWJD should be better understood as "What *Will* Jesus Do?" so that He becomes the Author of His own activity from within the believer. Even the acronym for GRACE should be augmented to go beyond – "God's Riches at Christ's Expense" to include "God's Resources (for) Any Christian Expression". We are saved by *grace through faith* and we are to live the Christian life *by grace through faith*. Look at it again. *"…and the life I now live, I live by faith … I do not frustrate the grace."* – Galatians 2:20, 21. That is the secret of being the believer you have become.

By the way, go back to the seaside multitude for just a moment. When the disciples respond to Christ's command with their own insufficiency Jesus takes over. He asks an innocent question – *"What do you have? Go and see."* John's account fills in the gaps and a little boy is brought to Andrew who in turn brings him to Jesus to reveal a small lunch of five loaves and two fishes. Peter is looking over his shoulder and snickers, "I can eat more than that!"

Jesus turns to Peter in a more serious tone and says something to the effect of "Simon, why don't you make yourself useful and find a basket." Peter scoffs to himself, "Why? It came in a bag."

Jesus ignoring the comment He wasn't supposed to hear turns to the rest of the disciples and announces, "And the rest of you – find some baskets …. We're going to need them!"

Then taking the five loaves and two small fishes, He holds them up towards heaven and prays, "Thank you Father, for what *You* are about to do!"

Then taking the fish and bread, He begins to break them into pieces until He fills one of the baskets. Handing the basket to Peter, He says firmly, "Get them seated in groups of fifty and a hundred and Peter, I want you to take that group *right over there!*"

That is missions! When God fills our basket, points us to a people group and says, "now give them what I have given you!" Immediately, Peter gathers his group and begins passing out the food. When he empties his basket, he realizes that he has barely made a dent in the numbers and begins walking back to the Master thinking to himself what many of us have said aloud in the face of an overwhelming task – "I knew this wasn't going to work!"

But when he arrives to drop his basket at Jesus' feet, Jesus is still breaking bread, still filling baskets. He turns to Peter and says, "Take your basket, get at the end of the line, and I'll get back to you in a minute!"

He sends him out again … and again, and somewhere around the sixth or seventh trip out Peter realizes, "This is fantastic! I never thought when I got up this morning that I would be part of something like this!" Jesus has given the disciples the two things they needed to feed a multitude – desire and ability. That is *Grace*!

By the way … isn't that the way you want to live your life?

– Chapter Four –

"The Two Comforters"
[John 14:11-14]

> *"Believe Me that I am in the Father and the Father in Me, or else believe Me for the sake of the works themselves. Most assuredly, I say to you, he who believes in Me, the works that I do he will do also; and greater works than these he will do, because I go to My Father.*
>
> *And whatever you ask in My name, that I will do, that the Father may be glorified in the Son. If you ask anything in My name, I will do it.*   **John 14:11-14**

Jesus said the evidence of His relationship with the Father was to be found in His works. In like manner, the evidence of our relationship will be seen in our works. This is not to say that our works earn us a relationship with Him any more than my works earned me a place into the Pool family. In fact, it was the work of my parents that got me into the family in hopes that I would not disgrace the name of the family by my works. We are not *born* of works, but of God. But we are *born* for works wrought *by* God – for without Him, we could do *nothing*. But with Him we can do *"greater works than these"* performed by Jesus Himself. How can that be? I suspect it has something to do with *His name*.

IN MY NAME

Between John 14:13 and 16:27, the phrase *"in my name"* or *"for my name"* appears no less than eight times. In John 17, Jesus speaks of *"Your name"* referring to the Father four separate times in twenty verses. Listed below are the scriptures (New King James Version).

- *And whatever you ask **in My name**, that I will do, that the Father may be glorified in the Son. If you ask anything **in My name**, I will do it.* **John 14:13, 14**
- *But the Helper, the Holy Spirit, whom the Father will send **in My name**, He will teach you all things, and bring to your remembrance all things that I said to you.* **John 14:26**
- *You did not choose Me, but I chose you and appointed you that you should go and bear fruit, and that your fruit should remain, that whatever you ask the Father **in My name** He may give you.* **John 15:16**
- *But all these things they will do to you **for My name's** sake, because they do not know Him who sent Me.* **John 15:21**
- *And in that day you will ask Me nothing. Most assuredly, I say to you, whatever you ask the Father **in My name** He will give you. Until now you have*

> *asked nothing **in My name**. Ask, and you will receive, that your joy may be full. John **16:23, 24***

- *In that day you will ask **in My name,** and I do not say to you that I shall pray the Father for you; **John 16: 26***
- *"I have manifested **Your name** to the men whom You have given Me out of the world. They were Yours, You gave them to Me, and they have kept Your word. **John 17:6***
- *Now I am no longer in the world, but these are in the world, and I come to You. Holy Father, keep **through Your name** those whom You have given Me, that they may be one as We are. While I was with them in the world, I kept them **in Your name**. Those whom You gave Me I have kept; and none of them is lost except the son of perdition, that the Scripture might be fulfilled. **John 17:11, 12***
- *And I have declared to them **Your name**, and will declare it, that the love with which You loved Me may be in them, and I in them." **John 17:26***

The significance of this expression is much greater than we have given to it by merely tacking it onto the end of our prayers as though it were a heavenly zip code. It is not a mystical expression or a required closing to indicate the completion of a supplication. It is a vital condition to our prayer.

By the way,… we can pray "in His name" without saying "*in Jesus' name*". Truth be known, more prayers use that expression in vain more than in earnest, because it is often recited under pressure of expectation on the part of others listening. God knows if we are praying "in Jesus' name" by the beginning of the prayer – not the ending.

What does it mean to be "in His name"? The different scriptures in this passage shed light on its meaning. It is true that six of the examples involve asking, but one involves the Father sending and one involves persecution. To help get a handle on the expression, let me share a story from Honduras.

As a church planter in the southern region of Honduras, I spent many days at a time away from home visiting villages. While staying in a rural village, I would get to know many of the merchants as well as the church members of a community. Occasionally, the two would overlap.

I remember a particular community where a local store was owned and operated by a sister from the local Baptist Church where I would be conducting classes or workshops. Maria, the owner, would say to me, "anytime you want a cold drink, just let me know and I will send one over at no charge." I didn't abuse her generosity, but on occasion, I would get dry speaking and a cold soft drink was just the thing to keep me going.

One hot afternoon, I found myself parched and in need of a cold drink. I asked one of the young men to run over to Maria's and ask her for a soft drink and to bring it back as quickly as possible. While he was gone, I was asked the question about praying "in Jesus' name". As I began to explain, the young man returned and handed me the open bottle. I looked at it for a moment and then asked the young student a couple questions before he sat down.

"Jose, did you have any trouble getting the drink?" I asked.

"No *hermano* (brother), she didn't hesitate," he said proudly.

"Did she charge you for the drink?" I asked.

"No sir, she said it was free," he smiled at me and then at the class.

"Has she ever given you a free drink before?" I then asked.

"No sir, she is kind, but she must run her business," he explained. The class laughed in agreement.

"But she didn't hesitate to give you a drink and not charge you today," I ventured.

"Yes sir, … but it wasn't for me," he clarified.

"What do you mean?" I asked. "She gave it to *you* didn't she?"

Jose smiled bigger. He knew what I was saying, so he played along.

"She gave it to me to give to you," he said firmly.

"Well, let me ask you this then," I began pacing back and forth. "Why did you go for the drink in the first place?"

"Because you asked me to go," he answered slowly.

"And what did you say when you got to Maria's?" I probed.

"*Hermano Randy* would like a cold drink," he responded recalling his own words.

"Did she ask you 'why'?" I pressed.

"No, she just gave me the drink and I brought it to you," he said.

"Let me get this straight then," I recapped. "I wanted a cold drink, I asked you to get me a cold drink. You asked for a cold drink for me and she gave you a cold drink. And now I can enjoy this cold drink."

"Yes sir," that is what just happened.

Turning to the class I explained. "Jose just got a free cold drink *in my name*. He went at my command, he asked using my authority, and he received for my benefit. She did not do it for him, she did it for me. Any questions?"

The light came on. To ask *in Jesus' name* is not to get what we want, but to receive what He wants us to use for His glory. That is how the Father sent the Spirit *in His name*. He did so at the request of the Son, in the shared authority with the Son, for the glory of the Son. That is why the world will persecute us *for His name* - because we come at the command of Jesus, identified with the person and purpose of Jesus, for the glory of Jesus. If they hated Him, they will hate us as well (John 15:18-20).

In His name becomes another way of understanding "in Him". In Him, we have our identity, our authority and our justification. What a comfort to know that we are not asking on our own for ourselves. And yet the One in whom we ask is no longer with us in person. He has ascended to the right hand of the Father to be our "Advocate" with the Father. So where is the presence of His name? That presence now dwells *in* us. That presence gives to us our relationship with the Father, our power for transformation, and grace for obedience. All is made possible by the same person – *the other Comforter.*

The Other Comforter – The Holy Spirit

He is mentioned and identified in chapters 14, 15, and 16.

- *And I will pray the Father, and He will give you another Helper* (Comforter), *that He may abide with you forever – the Spirit of truth, whom the world cannot receive, because it neither sees Him nor knows Him; but you know Him, for He dwells with you and will be in you.* **John 14:16, 17**
- *But the Helper* (Comforter), *the Holy Spirit, whom the Father will send in My name, He will teach you all things, and bring to your remembrance all things that I said to you.* **John 14:26**
- *"But when the Helper* (Comforter) *comes, whom I shall send to you from the Father, the Spirit of truth who proceeds from the Father, He will testify of Me.* **John 15:26**

- *Nevertheless I tell you the truth. It is to your advantage that I go away; for if I do not go away, the Helper (Comforter) will not come to you; but if I depart, I will send Him to you.* **John 16:7**

From these verses, we can draw some important insights concerning the person and role of the Holy Spirit.

- He is "*another*" Comforter making Him equal to the "first" Comforter. The term "another" is the Greek term used for "another of the same kind". The word "comforter" is the same word used to describe Jesus in 1 John 2:1 - "*And if anyone sins, we have an **Advocate** with the Father, Jesus Christ the righteous.*" Both are "Paraclete" ("one called alongside").
- He is the *permanent* presence of God *in* the believer (John 14:16, 17) In the Old Testament, the Holy Spirit came "*upon*" people and would come and go.
- He is that which separates believers from the world (John 14:17). The Holy Spirit makes a distinction between the believer and the unbeliever and becomes the means for *knowing* God (*Him).*
- He is not just the *power* of God, He is the *person* of God. We can *know* Him. (John 14:17). As the person of God acting upon man, the Holy

Spirit becomes the "change agent" that works grace through the believer.

- He will *teach* the believer (John 14:26) - Receiving the Holy Spirit does not make one suddenly a "super Saint", but rather equips one to be "conformed" into the image of Jesus Christ through a process of transformation whereby one develops godly character.

- He will *glorify Christ* in and through the believer. The chief role of the Holy Spirit is to reproduce the character of Christ in the Child of God and in so doing fill the land with the "glory of God". Everything the Spirit stirs points to Christ. He does not seek his own glory and will not draw attention to himself.

In addition, the Holy Spirit has a role to play in the life of the unbeliever as well.

> *"And when He has come, He will convict the world of sin, and of righteousness, and of judgment: of sin, because they do not believe in Me; of righteousness, because I go to My Father and you see Me no more; of judgment, because the ruler of this world is judged."* **John 16:8**

To "reprove" is to expose or "bring to light". The three areas of exposure are sin, righteousness and judgment. Each of these relates to the unbeliever (the world) and is employed to draw the unbeliever to Jesus. That is the work of the Holy Spirit.

The conviction of the Holy Spirit is God's reproof of sin. It is the Holy Spirit that convinces man from within what his mind rejects. Debates over depravity fall short of conviction. The role of conviction is not to condemn but to draw the individual to a point of repentance based on truth (righteousness). The Holy Spirit presents both. He presents the true righteousness of God in the nature of Jesus Christ and the true sinfulness of man in the nature of Adam. Such conviction is found in the grace God extends to all. When genuine conviction is embraced (by faith), the sinner desires forgiveness and reconciliation with God.

The Spirit will expose genuine righteousness to the unbeliever through the works of the believer. Genuine righteousness is that which has its origin in God. "Dead works" are often mistaken for "good works", but lack the divine activity that brings genuine glory to God. Only the Spirit can engage man in acts of righteousness as the presence of God in the believer. Only the Spirit can demonstrate to the unrighteous what true righteousness is. Without the Spirit there is no righteousness. The Spirit will expose the false with the truth. That is how He (The LORD) will judge the world "in righteousness" (Psalm 9:8).

Finally the Spirit will expose the works of Satan (the prince of this world) in judgment (*krisis*). By doing this, the world will know the origin of its works of unrighteousness. The purpose of this judgment is to draw the unbeliever to the "Light" – the same Light used to expose the works of darkness (John 3:19-21). The word translated *"condemnation"* (verse 19) is the same word translated *"judgment"* in John 16:8.

Jesus was the first "Comforter" in the flesh. The Holy Spirit is the second "Comforter" Who has been granted access to the human spirit through the work of redemption and regeneration. It is this second *comforter* that makes the presence of the first *comforter* real in our experience and life. It is the second *comforter* Who will lead us into all truth and guide us … by the Way.

– Chapter Five –

The Two "Little Whiles"
[John 16:16]

"A little while, and you will not see Me; and again a little while, and you will see Me, because I go to the Father." **John 16:16**

By the way … on the road to the garden, Jesus stops again in a vain attempt to alert His disciples to what he had been trying to tell them for nearly a year. They didn't want to hear it then and they were still unprepared to hear it now. This explains why Jesus tried to keep the disciples quiet about who He was… even when they knew.

I have mentioned Peter's "confession of faith" found in Matthew 16. Let's take a closer look. Somewhere in the final months of Jesus' ministry, he and the disciples found themselves in Caesarea Philippi. The reputation of this Galilean had flourished to a point of extreme notoriety. It is Jesus who initiates the conversation with a probing question, "Who do the people say that I am?" The disciples respond enthusiastically. One shouts out, "Elijah!" One exclaims, "Jeremiah, or one of the other prophets!" One even mentions that, "some say you are

John the Baptist!" which is ironic, because John has been executed by this time and for Christ to have been John the Baptist, he would have had to rise from the dead. Not to mention the fact that they were cousins and He himself had been baptized by this same John.

This led Jesus to dig a little deeper and to assess their opinion of Him.

"Who do *you* say that I am?" he asked.

Without hesitation, Peter stepped forward. "You are the Christ (*the Anointed One – the Messiah*), the Son of the Living God!" he declared.

In one of those rare moments when a disciple actually *"got it right"*, Jesus turns … looks Peter square in the eyes and announces proudly, *"Very Good, Peter! … full marks! You are absolutely right!* 'Blessed are you, Simon Bar-Jonah, for flesh and blood has not revealed *this* to you, but My Father who is in heaven.' *You have been listening to my Father for a change!"*

Suffice it to say, Peter was commended for his "profession of faith". What is oftentimes missed is the command that followed the blessing - *"Then He commanded His disciples that they should tell no one that He was Jesus the Christ.* (vs. 20). Why? Although they now knew He was the Christ, the Son of the Living God – they had no idea what that meant. The Messiah was to deliver Israel and they were currently under Roman occupation. The natural conclusion was that Jesus would somehow break the yoke of their oppressors. Then Jesus revealed to them the next step in His divine mission – "From that time Jesus began to show to His disciples that He must go to Jerusalem, and suffer many things from the elders and chief priests and scribes, and be killed, and be raised the third day" (vs. 21).

Talk about confused. How could He be the Messiah and yet be killed by the religious order of His own people? Peter stepped forward again to correct the Master. Scripture indicates that he did so sternly by *rebuking* Him – to which Jesus replied in kind by shunning Peter in front of them all. He then declared as strongly as he had just moments before, "*Get behind Me, Satan! You are an offense to Me, for you are not mindful of the things of God, but the things of men.*" You see, it does no good to know *Who* Jesus is if you do not accept *why* He came and *what* He did. It is not enough to believe that Jesus is the "*Christ (Messiah), the Son of the Living God*", if you do not embrace (by faith) His atoning death and his glorious resurrection. Loyalty to the *person* of Jesus is not the same as obedience to the *will* of Jesus. You can have the correct doctrine and know Who He is and not know Him well enough to know His will for your life. You cannot say, "*Not so Lord!*" If He is Lord – you can't tell Him *no!* If you tell Him no – then He is not *Lord*.

Back along the way,… Jesus has perplexed them again with his statement, "*A little while, and you will not see Me; and again a little while, and you will see Me, because I go to the Father.*" The passage indicates that they had no idea what he meant, and He knew it.

Jesus tries to explain without spelling it out. He had been perfectly clear in Matthew 16 and they didn't want to hear it. They did not want the cross and up to this point they didn't understand the resurrection. They had never preached the Gospel that you and I have come to accept and believe so readily because it hadn't happened yet and they weren't looking for it. It would take four more days and an empty tomb for their understanding to be opened. But make no mistake, Jesus is speaking here of his death, burial and resurrection.

"A little while" and I will be dead, buried and gone. You will *"weep and lament"* but the world that did not want me here, the world that will have thought that they had finally gotten rid of me will *"rejoice"* … because I will be gone and *"you will not see me"*.

But then *"a little while and your sorrow will be turned to joy"* because I will return to you and you *"will see me again"*. It won't take long … just three days and I will be back with you and then *"no one will be able to take your joy away!"*.

Without ever mentioning the cross, his death, his burial or his resurrection, Jesus has prepared them for what would happen in the next four days – just two *"little whiles"* away. Those two brief periods of waiting are the reason He came, the reason he lived among them, poured his life into them, so that he could pour out his life for them and provide a life they could never know apart from him.

In the midst of explaining what a relationship with him would look like, he pauses long enough to share how such a relationship would be made possible. He was about to die for them, whether they understood that or not. He was about to rise from the dead, whether they believed that or not. He was about to rip apart the veil that separated sinful man from a Holy God and provide a Way to the Father. And he couldn't tell them in terms plain enough to understand.

Such it is with the Gospel. It is not as simple a matter to share as we might think. I suppose that is why we have devised clever acronyms and simple plans to present the greatest news that anyone could ever receive. If we are not careful, we will only produce the same confusion that the disciples experienced that night.

The sharing of the Gospel is quite different than presenting *"How to Receive Eternal Life"* or *"How to have your Sins Forgiven"* or even *"How to Become a Christian and Know that You are Going to Heaven When You Die"*. We are more inclined to present the benefits of salvation than we are the Savior Himself. Please understand that *no one will ever enter heaven accepting a plan*. The Gospel is about receiving *a Man – Jesus Christ*!

Peter didn't want to accept that Christ had to die. He couldn't understand how that could possibly effect a change in the world around him. He was only looking with human eyes and listening with human ears – so Jesus rebuked him for not *"minding the things of God"* but rather *"minding the things of man"*. When we share the Gospel, we must do so while *"minding the things of*

God". Salvation is not just about what *man* gets out of the arrangement, but also what *God* gets out of it.

We do not lead people to pray to receive forgiveness without repentance and confession of sin. We do not lead people to pray for eternal life without them understanding that eternal life is to "know God and Jesus Christ, whom he has sent" (John 17:3). We do not lead people to pray for a home in heaven without explaining that God desires a home in them as well. There is no salvation without receiving *Jesus Christ* Himself. There is no Gospel without His death, burial and resurrection.

Jesus *had to die* and so must we. We must die to self in order to live *with* Him. We must accept *that* if we are to receive him. The message of the Gospel is a figure (a portrait) of our own entrance into the Kingdom of God. As Paul later explains to the Romans and the Galatians, we have been "crucified with Christ" and have "died to sin". We have been "buried with Him by baptism into death" and "raised with him to walk in a newness of life". His passion has become ours. It takes more than repeating a prayer – it takes repenting of a heart of sin and placing ones complete trust in the God who made me ... to save me. And it can happen in just "*a little while*".

The First "Little While" –

The first "*little while*" was upon them. The night was falling fast around the small group and yet there was still much to take place. First, he would pray with them (John 17) and then he would separate himself from the group to pray and agonize alone (Gethsemane). Judas would come with a small army to take him. He would be dragged before the High Priests Annas and Caiaphas (just as he predicted) to be beaten, mocked and arraigned by an illegal court. During this time, Peter will follow from a distance and ultimately deny him three times. He will realize what he had done and leave Jesus alone with his captors to lament his own personal failure.

When the sun rises on that High Feast Day, Jesus is carried to Pilate, the Roman governor, before whom it would be necessary for the Jews to have Jesus publicly crucified, since their laws only allowed for stoning. Pilate will try to pass the responsibility to a Jewish figure head, Herod claiming the Galilean needed a local judicial judgment, but soon finds Jesus back on his portico. He makes two further attempts to release himself from the decision that his wife warned him against from a disturbing dream she had recently. The first attempt was to have him beaten beyond recognition hoping that the Roman cruelty would satisfy the blood-lust of the Jewish religious leaders. It only excited them to frenzy. When offered a choice between a convicted murderer and seditionist or this itinerate blasphemer, the priests convinced the crowd to call for the release of the murderer.

In a physical state of exhaustion and trauma and an emotional state of rejection and abandonment,

Jesus was both further humiliated and tortured with rods and thorns. Forced to carry his own instrument of destruction, he made his way through the painful pathway that led to Golgotha while being both cheered and jeered by the taunting crowd that had no idea who he was or why he was about to die.

Should I stop? There is more … much more. The next three hours would be the longest and darkest hours that any man, any angel, and any demon would ever know. God the Father turned his face from God the Son and He who knew no sin became sin for you and for me. No theology can adequately describe what those three hours must have been like. What may have seemed like "*a little while*" on the cross was an eternity for the Eternal One. When there is no concept of time, even "*a little while*" separated from the Father is too much. That was the price he came to pay. He took an "eternity" of separation from His Father and endured it for you and for me.

His disciples scattered and ironically, it was two religious leaders (Nicodemus and Joseph of Arimathea) that claimed the corpse, wrapped and anointed the body and buried him in a "borrowed" tomb. For the next three days, the Jews would continue to feast, to celebrate and to rejoice over their Passover – not realizing that they had just slaughtered the Lamb slain from the foundation of the world. His disciples would mourn behind locked doors - at least for "*a little while*".

The Second "Little While" –

Whereas the first *"little while"* would take less than twenty-four hours to pass, the second *"little while"* would require three days and three nights. The Bible is replete with references of three days.

- Three days journey for Abraham and Isaac to Mount Moriah – Genesis 22
- Three days for the baker and butler to receive their judgment from Pharaoh - Genesis 40.
- Three days for Israel to journey from Egypt into the wilderness to worship their God – Exodus 3
- Three days of darkness over the land of Egypt during the ninth plague – Exodus 10
- Three days journey from the mountain of the Lord – Numbers 10
- Three days notice for crossing over the Jordan under Joshua – Joshua 1
- Three days hiding for the spies to escape from Jericho – Joshua 2
- Three days puzzling over a riddle by Samson – Judges 14
- Three days David hid waiting for Jonathon to determine if it was safe – 1 Samuel 20
- Three days of plague on Israel for David's sin of counting the people – 2 Samuel 24
- Three days that Nehemiah surveyed the conditions of Jerusalem – Nehemiah 2

- Three days the people prayed and fasted with Esther before she entered before the King – Esther 4
- Three days and three nights Jonah spent in the belly of the great fish – Jonah 1

It was that last account which Jesus referenced concerning his death, burial and resurrection – which has led some to believe that Jonah actually died and was raised from the dead by God while in the belly of the whale. At the very least, it moves the crucifixion to Thursday as John's gospel would suggest by naming the Sabbath as the High Feast Day of the Passover and not the seventh day of the week as is commonly inferred. Regardless of the weekday upon which Jesus was crucified, the resurrection was without dispute – the first day of the week – three days later.

The women came first. They had hoped to anoint the body, though that had already been done by Joseph and Nicodemus. They wondered how they would move the heavy stone that kept the world out, but couldn't keep the Son of God in. Their wonders turned to wonder as they found the stone rolled away. Bewildered Romans fled, while believing women ran to find the men that should have been watching for what their Master had predicted on so many occasions. But as was noted earlier, at that time they neither understood the cross nor believed in the resurrection – even when the women told them.

They found the disciples behind locked doors and only two ventured out to prove they were just "silly women" spouting "idle tales". Is it a wonder the world has trouble believing when his own men were slow to accept the truth of the resurrection. What so many of us take on faith, they struggled with "face to face". Perhaps it was because the resurrection had to be more than just a story for them. It had to be real! Their lives depended on it. The resurrection was more than a doctrine – it was living proof that what the disciples had just experienced had meaning. More than that, it was the assurance that the previous three years were just a prelude to a life that none of them could imagine.

The resurrection was to become the foundation of the apostolic preaching because it validated the crucifixion. Martyrs came and went. It was little to die for a cause. It was something to rise from the dead for it. What's more, the resurrection was not just a resuscitation. Jesus did not rise from the grave as the widow's son, Jairus' daughter or even Lazarus. They would die again. Jesus rose to ever live – to return to the Father and take His place upon the throne forever.

The resurrection must become more than a part of the church pageant if it is to make a difference in our lives today. We give a standing ovation to the white robed actor of the Passion Play who appears above the "empty tomb" at the crescendo of our Easter Musical and then live defeated lives denying the power of that resurrection in our personal experience. The resurrection was the central truth of first century preaching and we act as though everyone already knows and accepts its validity. The resurrection is too special to be relegated to simple history – it was and is *His Story*!

The difference between Christ's resurrection and Greek Mythology is becoming blurred by postmodern indifference and apathy. If we do not live in the relevance of the resurrection, how can we expect to speak of it with any conviction? The fact of the resurrection cannot be separated from the *act* of the resurrection. Like the disciples who witnessed it, *our lives depend upon it!* Have I made it clear yet that this truth is indispensable to your relationship to God and its proclamation is indispensable to your witness? There is *no* Gospel without the death, burial and *resurrection* of Jesus Christ!

– Chapter Six –

The Two Prayers
[John 17]

> *"I pray for them. I do not pray for the world but for those whom You have given Me, for they are Yours."* **John 17:9**
>
> *"I do not pray for these alone, but also for those who will believe in Me through their word;"* **John 17:20**

The twenty-six verses of John seventeen is truly the "Lord's Prayer". What we memorized as children from Matthew six has been properly labeled the "Model Prayer". It was given to show us *how* to pray. You want to hear the heart of our Lord, tune into John seventeen. Though recorded on the eve of his crucifixion, this *is not* Gethsemane! He won't reach the garden until the next chapter. This is the prayer that Jesus prays in the presence of *all* of his disciples to underscore what he has been teaching them for the past three chapters. There is no anguish in these words. There is no "cup" to be passed, nor "will" to be surrendered. This is not the beginning of the Suffering. That time is soon, but for these twenty-six verses, Jesus is going to pray for two groups. He is going to pray two requests for both groups. He is going to pray for their unity and for their activity. He is going to move his final instructions from being relational to being missional.

The time had come. From the moment of His first miracle, Jesus reminded those around him that His life was moving toward a purpose that was defined in scope and timing. He told his mother at the wedding of Cana that his hour had not yet come (John 2:4). On at least two occasions in John, those wishing to do him harm were refrained *because His hour had not yet come* (John 7:30, John 8:20). That hour had knocked on the door with the coming of the Greeks to worship at the Passover and to see Jesus (John 12:20-27). That final meal which started this whole discourse marked the beginning of that hour that Jesus had been awaiting his entire life (John 13:1). The hour of the Passover was the hour of the Passion – the hour for which He came – and that hour had come!

Before we look at his two prayers, take a careful look at his opening request – *"glorify Your Son, that the Son also may glorify you!"* How was God the Father to *glorify* God the Son? It helps to understand that the purpose of *glory* is to manifest (or bring to light) the nature and character of God Himself (John 17:6). We were created to *reflect His glory*. For God to *glorify the Son* was to manifest the nature of God *through* His Son in his upcoming passion. Jesus is praying that God will reveal to man what His death, burial and resurrection was about to accomplish. In so doing, Jesus would be manifesting the nature and character of His Father in *redemption*, which was the purpose of his coming. By the Father *bringing to light* what the Son was about to do – the Son would be *bringing to light* what the Father had set out to accomplish through the Son's coming.

The second comment worth mentioning concerns *eternal life*. Without a clear understanding of *eternal life*, we may find ourselves evangelizing the masses towards the wrong conclusion. If I were to ask you to formulate a definition for *eternal life*, I suspect I would receive concepts of heaven or being forever in the presence of God. For most, the idea of *eternal life* and *afterlife* are closely aligned suggesting that *eternal life* is something that happens after you die. Some may even gravitate to the emphasis being on *life* rather than *eternal*, because after all, even those consigned to hell will live eternally. But that still does not describe the nature of that life. For some, it is eternal rest with no external hardships (tears, pain, sickness, sorrow, etc.). For some, it is eternal enjoyment (including family reunions, getting to know saints from centuries past, praise, singing, worship, etc.). For some, it may include getting all of their questions answered, and all of their mysteries explained. Whatever the concept, that becomes the motivation for wanting *eternal life*. But what does God say about *eternal life*? If our concepts differ, are we really seeking the same thing?

Jesus offers a Biblical definition for *eternal life* in John 17: 3. Hear his words, *"And this is eternal life, that they may know You, the only true God, and Jesus Christ whom You have sent."* I can't tell you how many people I have heard excited about going to heaven, but are not very interested in spending time with God *now*. They have very little interest in prayer, Bible study, or even spending time with God's people. They demonstrate very little interest in the matters that weigh heavy on God's heart – and yet, they look forward to spending an eternity in a place that He is preparing. We must remind ourselves – *if there is a mansion with my name on it, it is <u>in</u> my Father's House – not across the field where I can keep to myself.* The truth is, the word is "dwelling place" and not "mansion". God isn't building something for me to enjoy apart from Him, He is making room for me *where he is*!

Eternal life is knowing God. It begins the moment we enter into a relationship with Him through Jesus Christ. It is that incredible connection that is only made possible through the forgiveness of sins and restoration of the Spirit that was lost through Adam's fall. It is the intimate communion of fellowship that is shared between creator and creation. It is not knowing that God exists – it is knowing the God that exists.

It is not only the *one true God* that we come to know, but *his Son Jesus Christ whom he has sent* as well. It is the second part of that definition that leads us into his two prayers. Jesus was sent to do more than provide the *Way* – he also came to communicate that way to those who would hear him. He was sent to incarnate God's love to man. In the verses that follow, he is about to pass that baton onto his disciples.

The First prayer – John 17:9-19

Christ's first petition was for his disciples – specifically those within earshot of his prayer. He affirms God's work in their life and their response to that work (John 17:6-8). They know that Jesus was sent by God – even if they were not clear why. They had received his word as the Word of God that it was. They believed (at least) that Jesus had come from the Father.

He begins his prayer by distinguishing between those who have a personal relationship with him through the father and those who do not – the world. I am aware that this conversation could slip into election and since that is not my intention, I will simply say, there is a distinction between those who know him and those who do not. This prayer is for the believer – enough said.

Though there is a distinction between *who* they are – there is no distinction between the *where* they are. There are two understandings of the *world* in this prayer. There is the "world" that does not know God and there is the "world" in which we all live. One is a spiritual realm and the other is our physical realm. The best distinction of the two concepts are the expressions "in the world" and "of the world". We are "in the world" (physically), but we are not to be "of the world" (spiritually). In the physical realm, Jesus is "no longer in the world" (verse 11) because the hour has arrived for him to leave. His disciples on the other hand are "in the world" and will continue to be so after his departure. He then turns his attention to their relationship to the Father and to one another. The prayer for the disciples becomes multi-faceted.

> *Prayer for unity* – "…that they may be one as We *are*." *John 17:9-11*

Oneness is a quality of God that defies understanding. How God can be three in one has never been fully understood, let alone explained. When Christ declared *"I and the Father are one"* (John 10:30), he stated one of the greatest mysteries of life – how deity could share in humanity with an equality that was both singular and distinctive. Now he was praying for that kind of relationship among his followers. Not only that they should be united in purpose, passion, and perseverance, but that they should experience the same kind of oneness that the Father and Son shared. This could only be made possible if the divine spirit of both the Father and the Son were present in the believer. That is exactly what was about to take place, whether they realized it or not. The prayer for unity was a prayer that the disciples of Jesus Christ would receive the same *Spirit* that Christ himself possessed during his time on earth. This was a prayer based on what he had just taught them between the upper-room and where they presently stood.

The prayer for unity among the believers is the basis for the Church. It is to stand as a unified Body of Christ fulfilling and continuing the work of the Kingdom that was begun by the singular body of Christ that walked throughout Palestine and beyond preparing the world for the Gospel that he was about to perform. Their unity would be imperative to the role of the Church. Their unity would be the proof of his continued manifestation in the world. Their unity would make them more than a force to be reckoned with, it would make them the very "hands and feet" of the (soon to be) risen Lord.

This is the reason *fellowship* in the church in so much more than being entertained together – it is being intertwined together. The oneness of our purpose, the oneness of our prayers, the oneness of our praise constitutes the oneness of our spirits as we share in common His Spirit. Jesus prays that his disciples will know that kind of oneness and fellowship.

> *Prayer for Separation/ Sanctification* – "and the world has hated them because they are not of the world just as I am not of the world … Sanctify them by Your truth."
> *John 17:13–17*

As part of this oneness that they will share in fellowship with the Son, comes the persecution they will experience because of that oneness. Here Jesus begins to distinguish between being *in the world* and being *of the world*. He begins by speaking of the spiritual realm *of the world* hating them as they did Christ himself. The darkness will not enjoy fellowship with the light and we are foolish to think we can accomplish that. There will always be a separation between God and the world that no political position or motion can rectify. We can't make the world accept us when deep down by nature, it hates us. We can fight for our rights to co-exist, but that is not really our primary fight. Our battle is not to gain the acceptance of the world, but for the world to receive the acceptance of our Lord. Jesus and his disciples were not unclear on this matter:

- *Blessed are you when men hate you, And when they exclude you, And revile you, and cast out your name as evil, For the Son of Man's sake. Rejoice in that day and leap for joy! For indeed your reward is great in heaven, For in like manner their fathers did to the prophets.* Luke 6:22, 23
- *If the world hates you, you know that it hated Me before it hated you.*
  If you were of the world, the world would love its own. Yet because you are not of the world, but I chose you out of the world, therefore the world hates you. John 15:18,19
- *Do not marvel, my brethren, if the world hates you.* I John 3:13
- *And all who desire to live godly in Christ Jesus will suffer persecution.* 2 Timothy 3:12

> • *Beloved, do not think it strange concerning the fiery trial which is to try you, as though some strange thing happened to you; but rejoice to the extent that you partake of Christ's sufferings, that when His glory is revealed, you may also be glad with exceeding joy.* 1 Peter 4:12, 13

Jesus said they shall "separate you *from their company*". Our separation from the world is not just an altruistic effort to abstain from the sinful affairs of this age, but to realize that the unregenerate world doesn't desire the genuine things of the Kingdom and will oppose them at every opportunity. When the *world* is tolerant of the Church, it is usually an indication that the Church has compromised on some level. We are to be separate from the world (2 Corinthians 6:17) by not trying to be conformed to the world (Romans 12:2) but rather allowing the genuine nature of Christ to be seen in its glory through our lives. And when we do, the world will separate itself from us as well.

The irony of our separation is that it is *not* to be a physical separation from the world – "*I do not pray that You should take them out of the world, but that You should keep them from the evil one*" (verse 15). The monastery and commune approach to separation defeats the purpose for us to still be on this planet. God doesn't want to *protect* His people from the world, He wants to *infect* the world with His people. God wants to protect His people from the *evil one* (Satan) who is the origin of the world's system. When John speaks of all that is in the world (*1 John 2:15*) – "the lust of the flesh, the lust of the eyes and the pride of life", he is referring to the Satanic influence that deceived Eve in the garden and has blinded the eyes of man ever since.

Rather than take us out of the world, God desires that we take our place *in the world* as the rightful representatives of what mankind was supposed to look like re-created in the image of God through the transforming power of the indwelling Holy Spirit that has taken up residence in our human spirit to make us whole and complete. It is this new relationship with God that God wishes to share with all mankind and to do so He places us in the midst of those in need of that relationship.

Rather than send us back into the world in the same manner in which we were separated from it, Jesus now prays for our transformation through the process of sanctification – "*Sanctify them by Your truth. Your word is truth* (verse 17). Sanctification is the purpose for which we are set apart. Sanctification is the process whereby our lives become transformed "from glory to glory" (*2 Corinthians 3:18*) into the image of Jesus Christ – the purpose for which we were justified (*Romans 8:28*). Sanctification is being "saved by his life" (*Romans 5:10*) while we are still breathing. The means of that sanctification is by the Word of truth. The more we get to know God, the more we are in His presence, the more we see life from His perspective, the more we walk in the truth, the more sanctified we are becoming.

This changes the way others will see us. This leads us to the final aspect of Jesus' prayer for the believer.

> *Prayer for laborers to be sent* – "As You sent Me into the world, I also have sent them into the world." *John 17:18*

Here is where the transition moves from relational to missional. Up to this time, the emphasis has been on what kind of relationship Jesus would be having with those who would respond in repentance and faith to his upcoming work of redemption and justification. Reconciliation would provide the basis for regeneration. Regeneration would begin the process of transformation and sanctification – all of which being a result of coming to *know* God through His Son Jesus Christ and walking daily with him in spirit and truth. Now comes the responsibility side of this relationship. Justification is not just a gift that meets the righteous demands of a Holy God and grants access into His fellowship, it is basis from which God then exercises His authority over our lives and calls us into service. As Paul put it,

> *"For none of us lives to himself, and no one dies to himself. For if we live, we live to the Lord; and if we die, we die to the Lord. Therefore, whether we live or die, we are the Lord's. For to this end Christ died and rose and lived again,"* *Romans 14:7-9*

Salvation is not a one-sided gift. As stated in chapter one, "there is no mansion without a temple", "there is no Savior without a Lord", and here I would add, there is no relationship without responsibility. There is some truth in the adage "saved to serve". It is not just for those paid to do so in the ministry. In fact, more Kingdom work is realized through simple service than through vocational ministry. It is just a matter of finding your place in the fields.

Jesus called for laborers early on in His ministry. He chose twelve, sent out seventy, led multitudes and still called on prayer for more laborers – "*Then He said to His disciples, 'The harvest truly is plentiful, but the laborers are few. Therefore pray the Lord of the harvest to send out laborers into His harvest'*" (Matthew 9:37, 38). The question is not whether you are called to go – the question is where have you been sent? It is not a question of whether you have been sent – Jesus said, "*As You (the Father) sent Me into the world, I also have sent them into the world.*" I can hear the objections now. "But he was talking to the twelve!" Hold that thought. One thing is clear – Jesus has sent His disciples in the same manner that the Father had sent Him. In what way was Jesus sent? John gives us some examples:

- *He was sent on a mission with work to do –*
  John 4:34 - *Jesus said to them, "My food is to do the will of Him who sent Me, and to finish His work.*

- *He was sent as a physical representative of the Father -*
  John 5:23, 24 - *That all should honor the Son just as they honor the Father. He who does not honor the Son does not honor the Father who sent Him.*
  "Most assuredly, I say to you, he who hears My word and believes in Him who sent Me has everlasting life, and shall not come into judgment, but has passed from death into life."

- *He was sent with a message that was not His own -*
  John 7:16 - *Jesus answered them and said, "My doctrine is not Mine, but His who sent Me.*

- *He was sent to please the one Who sent Him -*
  John 8:29 - *And He who sent Me is with Me. The Father has not left Me alone, for I always do those things that please Him."*

- *He was sent to manifest the work/power of His Father –*
  John 9:4 - *I must work the works of Him who sent Me while it is day; the night is coming when no one can work.*

- *He was sent to be totally submissive to His Father –*
  John 13:16 - *Most assuredly, I say to you, a servant is not greater than his master; nor is he who is sent greater than he who sent him.*

- ***He was sent to be totally identified with His Father -***
  John 13:20 - *Most assuredly, I say to you, he who receives whomever I send receives Me; and he who receives Me receives Him who sent Me.*

In the same manner, Jesus sends out His disciples of whom we are included. How can I include us in that prayer? Because of his second prayer.

The Second Prayer – John 17:20-23

The second prayer was for YOU. I'm not kidding. Look at it again. If you are reading this book and you are a believer because of the words recorded by those who preached the gospel or other scriptures from which the good news of God's love was communicated you were covered by this prayer – *"I do not pray for these alone, but also for those who will believe in Me through their word,"* – John 17:20.

In short, everything Jesus just prayed for his disciples, he also prayed for you. The unity, the separation, the sanctification, the sending out … everything. He even draws the relationship of us in him and he in us within this prayer to bring us back to where this teaching all began. This prayer of intercession was shared aloud in the presence of his disciples, but it was recorded to be shared with all believers. This IS the Lord's prayer for his people. And he prayed it … on the way to the garden.

– Chapter Seven –

The One Conclusion
[John 17:24, 25]

"Father, I desire that they also whom You gave Me may be with Me where I am, that they may behold My glory which You have given Me; for You loved Me before the foundation of the world.

O righteous Father! The world has not known You, but I have known You; and these have known that You sent Me.

And I have declared to them Your name, and will declare it, that the love with which You loved Me may be in them, and I in them."

In the final words of his prayer of intercession for them and for us, Jesus pulls it all together. He speaks of the future predicated upon the past being realized by the present. Because of God's love before the foundation of the world, he is about to die for the sins of a fallen race of men, so that they might enjoy the glory of a relationship together for all eternity. By restoring that lost relationship, Jesus is making God known and *through* those to whom he restores he will continue declaring that same God throughout the nations that the *world* that opposed him might come to know that love and share in that relationship. It is about moving us from being relational *with* Christ – to being missional *with* Christ, because his desire is that we be *with him* … *where he is!* Knowing he was about to die, the only way he would continue to declare the name of God would be through his body that would remain *in the world* after his ascension to the Father. He has declared the name of God in person *and will* declare the name of God through us. The single conclusion of his discourse is …. *love.*

It is the love of God that put this entire plan into action. It is the love of God that prompted the Son to step out of eternity and into time. It is that same love that Jesus incarnated in life and ministry. It is that same love that Jesus extolled from the law and the prophets and then elevated among his disciples as the singular expression of obedience to a Holy God. It is that same love that he both demonstrated and demanded from his disciples in their relationships to both God and man. It is the same love that would hold his tongue when reviled, hold his cheek when smitten, hold his head up as it was crowned with thorns and ultimately hold his body to a cross as legions of angels waited biting their lips for the command of deliverance that he would never bid. It is that same love that flooded our hearts the moment we surrendered our self-centered will to the Lordship of the God of Love Himself. It is that same love that now constrains us to compel those we know and many we don't to discover that very love for themselves. It is a love relationship that bears a responsibility of love.

It is this love that the disciple recording this discourse revealed in one of the earliest moments of his remembrance with Jesus. It is this love that Jesus himself declared to a wayward theologian one night in a one-on-one encounter.

"For God so loved the world ….
   That he gave (sent) His One and only Son …
      That whoever believes in him (places their complete trust and dependence upon) …
         Shall not perish …(live a life separated from God)
            But have eternal life … (to know the One True God and Jesus Christ, His Son)

And having declared that love himself, he prepared a people through whom he would continue till this day declaring that love.

Such a message was important enough to interrupt a feast in order to explain. I trust this book has interrupted your dinner, because it is that important:

To know you are in Christ,…and that changes the way God sees you
To know Christ is in you,…and that changes the way the world sees you

To know you have a home in heaven *if* He has a home in you on earth,…

To know that you were saved for the *same* reason you were made,… to reflect the glory of God.

To know that you were reconciled by his death and are being saved by his life,…

To know that you submit to the Spirit that *dwells* in you rather than Him submitting to your requests,…

To know that as the Father sent the Son, The Son now sends you.

In short, as believers, we all have a relationship *and* a responsibility to Jesus Christ.

Hope to see you,…along the way!

ABOUT THE AUTHOR

Randy Pool is a believer, a husband and father, a missionary, and a storyteller. Born into a military family, his travels carried him to both coasts and Puerto Rico while still a young child. Then at the age of fifteen, his life was eternally changed by Jesus Christ.

Pursuant to a call to ministry, Randy received a BA degree in religion and Greek from Union University. He later earned his MDiv from Mid-America Baptist Theological Seminary of Memphis. While at Union, he met and married the love of his life, Cindy.

After ten years together, three children, and pastoring two churches, Randy and Cindy went to the mission fields of Central America. They served as church planters in Honduras and Nicaragua for eleven years with the International Mission Board of the Southern Baptist Convention.

Randy and Cindy now live back in Tennessee, where Randy serves with the Mississippi River Ministry, connecting churches to poverty areas within their community. He is still a missionary, now working through the Tennessee Baptist Convention. He sees writing as a channel of information, inspiration, as well as entertainment.

Randy has written for several Baptist publications, including Dimension Magazine, Missions Leader Magazine, Nuestra Tarea (Spanish Baptist Magazine), and the Baptist and Reflector (State newspaper). He has three other books in print, The Breach, The Bridge, and Poolside Reflections—all bearing the mark of missions.

Randy enjoys life. When time allows, he relaxes with family and friends in hammocks beneath a gallery built on their small homestead in Gibson County, a touch of Latin culture in West Tennessee. He enjoys telling stories that bring humor to life and Christ to heart.

ENDNOTES

1. Chapter 1- All quoted scriptures are taken from the New King James Version. Thomas Nelson Publishers. Nashville, TN. © 1994
2. Chapter 1 – "My Heart, Christ's Home" Robert Boyd Munger, InterVarsity Press Books; Expanded edition (February 20, 1986)
3. Chapter 3 - Amplified Bible, Zondervan Publishing House, Grand Rapids, Michigan; © 1965

Printed in the United States
By Bookmasters